Edward H Lisk

Representative Young Irish-Americans of Troy, N. Y.

Edward H Lisk

Representative Young Irish-Americans of Troy, N. Y.

ISBN/EAN: 9783337115418

Printed in Europe, USA, Canada, Australia, Japan

Cover: Foto ©ninafisch / pixelio.de

More available books at **www.hansebooks.com**

Edward H Lisk

Representative Young Irish-Americans of Troy, N. Y.

ISBN/EAN: 9783337115418

Printed in Europe, USA, Canada, Australia, Japan

Cover: Foto ©ninafisch / pixelio.de

More available books at **www.hansebooks.com**

REPRESENTATIVE

YOUNG IRISH-AMERICANS

OF TROY, N. Y.

1889.

FROM THE PRESS OF
E. H. LISK,
312 RIVER ST., TROY

The City of Troy.

It was in 1630 that Kiliaen Van Rensselaer, an Amsterdam pearl merchant, began to send emigrants to settle along the Hudson River. The West India Company had offered to any person belonging to the association who would induce fifty persons over fifteen years of age to settle within four years upon stated tracts of land in New Netherland, the title of patroon or proprietor of the land so settled. Van Rensselaer was ambitious to become a patroon, and in due time he was made patroon of Rensselaerwyck manor, a great stretch of territory now included in Rensselaer, Albany and Columbia Counties. The part of the manor upon which the city of Troy now stands was known on the earliest maps of the territory as the Pafraets Dael (Pafraets' part) so called in honor of Maria Pafraets, the mother of Kiliaen Van Rensselaer.

Lack of space prevents a detailed history of the early settlers hereabouts. Suffice it to say that when the first emigrants from New England came this way the site of Troy was in possession of three Dutch farmers. The farm lying between the Poestenkill and Division Street was owned by Matthias Van der Heyden, that between Division Street and Grand Street by Jacob D. Van der Heyden, and that between

Dennis J. Whelan.

Dennis J. Whelan.

DENNIS J. WHELAN, mayor of Troy, was born in Ireland September 1, 1846. He was brought to this country and to Troy when only four years old, and here he has ever since made his home. He was educated by the Christian Brothers. While serving his apprenticeship at the plumber's trade the civil war broke out. He was only a boy, but as time wore on and the North and the South came into more deadly conflict, he could not resist the patriotic impulse which fired his heart. He enlisted in the Twelfth New York Cavalry, Capt. Savage commanding, and served his country for two years At the close of the war Mr. Whelan finished his trade, and for twelve years thereafter worked steadily at it. In 1869 he married Miss Catherine Regan. The union proved a most happy one. In 1876 Mr. Whelan threw down his plumbers' tools and began the manufacture of soda water and other temperance drinks. This venture was successful. He is still in the business and occupies a large establishment at Nos. 104 and 106 Jefferson Street. In March, 1880, Mr. Whelan was elected an Alderman from the Eleventh Ward for the short term. He was reëlected in the fall of 1880, and was returned to the Common Council in 1882 and 1884. In March, 1882, he was chosen president of the Common Council. He was chosen again in 1884, and in 1885 was unanimously reëlected. the Republican minority supporting him most heartily, at that time an unheard of thing in local municipal affairs. While acting as president of the Common Council in 1885, the Quigley police force was legislated out of office, and by act of the Legislature the power to appoint the new commissioners was vested in Mr. Whelan. In 1886 he was chosen mayor and he has since held that office. The crowning act of his successful administration of municipal affairs came in the spring of 1889, when, through his patient efforts, a Citizens' Association was organized and a bill passed in the Legislature authorizing the expenditure of $850,000 for public improvement. The commission appointed by the mayor, in conformity with this act, gave universal satisfaction, and the gentlemen comprising the commission are now hard at work mapping out trunk sewers and pavements for the city. This year the sale of the city lots below the Poestenkill was authorized. Upon them are now in process of erection a new engine house and a new station house. A large public school building has been ordered erected in the Pawling Avenue district of the Fifth Ward. Mayor Whelan has been a successful man, and he possesses the confidence and respect of all classes of citizens.

William J. Roche.

William J. Roche.

WILLIAM J. ROCHE was born in this city in 1853. His parents were William Roche of Castletown Roche, County Cork, Ireland, and Margaret Guiry, a native of Bride Bridge, Parish of Castle Lyons, in the same county. William Roche came to this country in 1841 and Mrs. Roche in 1845. William J. Roche has always lived in Troy. After a thorough course at the Christian Brothers' Academy he commenced the study of law with Townsends & Browne. In 1878 he was admitted to the firm upon the retirement of Mr. Browne, and continued until the firm was dissolved in 1880. A new partnership was formed by Mr. Roche with Hon. Martin I. Townsend, which firm still exists. On Oct. 10, 1883, although barely thirty years old, Mr. Roche was appointed to the responsible and exacting position of city attorney. He discharged the duties of the office with marked ability, serving until February 7, 1886. He was appointed city comptroller December 21, 1886, to fill an unexpired term, and was appointed for the full term of three years January 29, 1887. Comptroller Roche took an active part in the movement which culminated in the passage of the Public Improvement Bill, and to him much of the success of the measure is due. He has codified the laws of the City of Troy, a bill covering which is pending in the Legislature. Comptroller Roche is a member of the Robert

Emmet Association and the Alumni Society of the Christian Brothers' Academy. Of each of these organizations he has twice served as president. He was married in 1880 to Miss Mary L. Campion, a native of New York City. They have four children, all boys, the oldest being seven years of age. Comptroller Roche has ever been actively interested in the meetings for the relief of distress in Ireland, and in aid of the Home Rule cause. He represented the Troy branch of the Irish National League of America in the national conventions of that body held in Philadelphia in 1883 and in Chicago in 1886.

John Francis Bridgeman.

John Francis Bridgeman.

JOHN F. BRIDGEMAN was born in this city Nov. 11, 1849.
He is the son of Peter and Mary Bridgeman. After a
thorough course in the public and the Christian Brothers'
schools he entered the store of Silliman, Matthews & Co.,
where he remained from 1866 to 1871. He was a salesman
for Graves, Page & Co., from 1872 to 1878, and in the latter
year he went into the wholesale grocery business under the
firm name of Taylor & Bridgeman. From 1879 until 1885
the subject of this sketch was a traveling salesman for
Barkhalter & Co. of New York. In 1885 he was appointed
city chamberlain, and so ably did he perform the exacting
duties of that important office that on the expiration of his
term he was reappointed. He has taken a prominent part in
the agitation for public improvement which has resulted in
the enactment of the Public Improvement Bill. Mr. Bridgeman is a member of the Robert Emmet Association and the
Commercial Travelers' Association of the State of New York.
He is also a trustee of the Pioneer Building and Loan Association. Mr. Bridgeman's wife was Kate C. Gillen. They
have one child, a bright boy of twelve.

Michael Francis Collins.

Michael Francis Collins.

MICHAEL F. COLLINS was born in this city Sept. 27, 1854. His parents were Patrick and Alice Collins. He has always resided in Troy. Mr. Collins was fortunate in his educational advantages, having attended the public schools and the Christian Brothers' Academy until thoroughly fitted for the real work of life. He learned the trade of compositor, working on the *Troy Weekly Press, Troy Sunday Telegram, Troy Daily Press* and *Troy Standard*. From 1869 until 1877 Mr. Collins worked assiduously at his trade. In the latter year he, with several associates, founded the *Troy Standard* and for two years was its efficient city editor. In 1879 he purchased the *Troy Observer*, which paper he has made one of the leading Democratic journals of the country. In 1886 he was elected Assemblyman from the First District of Rensselaer County, and the following year was reëlected by a largely increased majority. In the fall of 1888 he was nominated by the Democratic party for State Senator, and was elected, notwithstanding the fact that for years the district had been largely Republican. Mr. Collins is president of the famous Pilsner Democratic Club. He is married; his wife being Miss Carrie E. O'Sullivan. They have four children, two boys and two girls. Mr. Collins was a delegate to the Democratic State Convention in 1882 which nominated Grover Cleveland for Governor. He was also an alternate to the National Democratic Convention at Chicago in 1884, when Mr. Cleveland was named for the Presidency.

George O'Neil.

George O'Neil.

GEORGE O'NEIL was born in the Seventh Ward, this city, June 18, 1855, and has always resided in the same ward. He left the public schools in 1870 to accept a clerkship for Boardman Bros. He continued in their employ until 1880 when he went into the grocery business for himself at No. 42 King Street, where he remains to-day. In 1885, '86 and '87 he was chosen to represent the Seventh Ward in the Board of Supervisors. In 1887 he was elected a member of the State Assembly to represent the First Rensselaer District and the following year he was reëlected by a large majority. Mr. O'Neil has taken a very prominent part in shaping local legislation of late years, and both in business and political life he has attained a flattering success. He was married June 5, 1889, to Miss Sarah Kennedy.

John Joseph McCormick.

John Joseph McCormick.

JOHN J. McCORMICK, son of John and Mary Ann McCormick, was born in Brunswick, Rensselaer County, Nov. 23, 1849. His parents removed to Troy when the subject of this sketch was four years of age, and in this city he has since made his home. After a course at the Fifth Ward public school he entered the High School, where he made a fine record. For two years and a half Mr. McCormick was a clerk in W. W. Whitman's paper hanging establishment. Then he learned the carpenter's trade in the shop of W. J. Howes. For five years he worked as a journeyman for G. W. Oliver and other master builders. Later, for two years he was court clerk in the office of the Rensselaer County Clerk. He is at present book-keeper and cashier for the extensive brewing concern of Kennedy & Murphy. Mr. McCormick is city clerk. He has held that important position for several years with great credit to himself and satisfaction to his friends. For fourteen years he served as secretary of the Democratic General Committee. He was a delegate to the Democratic State Convention at New York in 1888, and a delegate to the Democratic Judiciary Convention at Albany in 1886. Among the civil offices he has held were the following: Treasurer of St. Francis' Church, president of the Y. M. C. L. A. Debating Society, president of the Mount Ida Dramatic Club and treasurer of the Mount Ida Benevolent Legion. Mr. McCormick's wife was Miss Johanna Cronin. They have two children, boys.

James W. Coffey.

James W. Coffey.

JAMES W. COFFEY was born in this city June 19, 1853. His parents were Michael and Sarah Coffey. James W. Coffey has resided here all his life. He received a splendid education under the direction of the Christian Brothers, and then entered the office of Runkle & Flagg. Later he was with Flagg & Neary, Neher & Calder and Thomas Neary. For Neher & Calder he was a book-keeper, and with the other firms a law clerk. He is now a practicing lawyer. He was the mayor's private secretary from 1882 until 1889, serving under Mayors Fitzgerald and Whelan. Mr. Coffey was appointed assistant police magistrate June 20, 1889, which position he now holds. From January, 1882, to January, 1883, he was president of the Robert Emmet Association. He is a member of the latter association, of the Catholic Benevolent Legion and of the Alumni Association of the Christian Brothers' Academy. He was married June 22, 1875, to Miss Nora A. Hartigan, daughter of ex-Supervisor Maurice Hartigan. He has four children, two boys and two girls.

Cornelius Hannan.

Cornelius Hannan.

CORNELIUS HANNAN was born Jan. 31, 1856, at Gateshead, County of Durham, England. His father was James Hannan and his mother Margaret Kiely, both of whom were born in Ireland. When Cornelius was very small his parents removed to this country and settled in West Troy. Later they moved to Saratoga County and there he remained for twenty-three years, coming to this city in 1881 from Ballston. Mr. Hannan obtained his education in the public schools of Ballston and at St. Mary's Academy, this city, from which he graduated in 1881. He entered the law office of Townsend & Roche in September of that year and was admitted to the bar just three years later. While residing in Saratoga County Mr. Hannan taught school and worked at farming. Mr. Hannan is a member of the Robert Emmet Association, and is one of the brightest young lawyers in the State. On Aug. 1, 1889, he was appointed private secretary to Mayor Whelan.

John J. Evers.

John J. Evers.

JOHN J. EVERS was born in this city June 1, 1848. His parents were Michael Evers and Mary Gaffigan. All of Mr. Evers' life has been spent in this city. After attending the Christian Brothers' Academy he learned the molder's trade and worked for Fuller, Warren & Co. and G. W. Swett & Co. He was employed ten years at his trade. For three years he was employed by his brother, Thomas F. Evers, and for two years held a United States government clerkship. At present he is the assistant clerk of the Board of Water Commissioners. For a number of years Mr. Evers was a member of the Board of School Commissioners, and he acted as president of that body. He has served as corresponding representative of Iron Molders' Union, No. 2. He is a member of the Union, a member of Byron Council, C. B. L., and a member of the Americus Club. His wife was Miss Ellen Keating, and he has seven children, four boys and three girls.

George Henry Mead.

George Henry Mead.

ALDERMAN GEORGE H. MEAD was born in this city June 12, 1853. His parents were John Mead and Mary Caufield. He received his education under the care of the Christian Brothers, and learned the trade of a cigarmaker at which he worked in various parts of the country. He served a term as president of the Cigarmakers' Union, No. 15, of New York. For ten years he was the foreman in W. A. Lent & Co.'s manufactory in this city. At present he is engaged in the hotel business. January 1, 1881, Alderman Mead was married to Miss Elizabeth Agnes Daigneault. For several years he has represented the First Ward in the Common Council, and for two years he was the presiding officer of that body. He is a member of Emerald Beneficial Association, the Exempt Firemen's Association, the Osgood Steamer Company, the Adonis Club, the Y. M. C. L. A., the Edward Murphy, Jr., Association (of which he is a trustee), and the Liquor Dealers' Association. He is an honorary member of the Cigarmakers' Union, No. 9, and has served as president of the Y. M. C. L. A. Alderman Mead is vice-president of the National League of Democratic Clubs, for the State of New York. He was an energetic member of the Centennial Committee of One Hundred, and is one of Troy's most promising young men.

William Holmes.

William Holmes.

WILLIAM HOLMES was born in this city December 20, 1848. His parents were William Holmes and Ellen Rainey. Mr. Holmes attended the Fourth Ward public school. He learned the trade of machinery molder at Starbuck's works and was engaged at his trade for nine years. In 1873 he went into the retail liquor business. In 1876 he was appointed on the detective force and remained in police service five years and nine months. Resigning from the force he associated himself with John F. Ahern in the retail liquor trade at No. 6 Third Street. Their present place of business is No. 12 Third Street. Mr. Holmes was president of the Liquor Dealers' Association for one year and vice-president for three years. He is now vice-president of the State organization. He is a member of the Pilsner Democratic Club, and has served as vice-president. For six years he was a member of the Board of School Commissioners. He is now a Fire Commissioner and president of the Board. For one term he was captain of the Ranken Steamer Company and for three years he was treasurer of the company. He is a member of the Exempt Firemen's Association. In 1875 he was a delegate to the Democratic State Convention at Syracuse. At present he represents the Fourth Ward in the Democratic General Committee. Mr. Holmes is also a member of the Y. M. C. L. A. He is married, his wife's maiden name being Miss Annie Smith. He has seven children.

John Patrick Curley.

John Patrick Curley.

ON NOV. 17, 1856, JOHN P. CURLEY was born in this city, and here he has always resided. His parents were Patrick and Margaret Curley. After attending the public schools and the parochial schools of the Sisters and Christian Brothers, Mr. Curley entered the law office of the late John H. Colby. In due time he was admitted to the bar. He served as a law clerk for about six years. Mr. Curley is serving his third term as Justice of the Justices' Court. On the bench he has been eminently successful. He has served as president and vice-president of the Y. M. C. L. A. and was president of the Bachelors' Club for two years. He is also a member of the A. O. H., Robert Emmet Association, Y. M. C. L. A., Bachelors' Club, Edward Murphy, Jr., Association and Pilsner Democratic Club. On Nov. 20, 1888, Mr. Curley was married to Mary A. V. Stanton, daughter of John Stanton. The subject of this sketch illustrates in his life the success which always rewards conscientious effort. Mr. Curley has a large legal practice, and is recognized as a leading member of the Rensselaer County bar.

John P. Kelly.

John P. Kelly.

JOHN P. KELLY was born in this city 29 years ago. He obtained his education in the public schools. In the offices of the late Thomas Neary and the late Judge E. Smith Strait, he studied law, and in 1881 was admitted to the bar. Mr. Kelly also worked in the Clinton foundry. He began the study of his profession when only 14 years old. In 1886 and '87 he was the attorney for the Board of Supervisors, and at the present time he is assistant district attorney of Rensselaer County. He was president of the Y. M. C. L. A. in 1886, and has been treasurer of the Edward Murphy, Jr., Association. Mr. Kelly was married in November, 1887, to Miss Ellen Fleming and has one child, a daughter.

John Edward Kelly.

John Edward Kelly.

JOHN E. KELLY was born in this city Feb. 11, 1863, his parents being Edward and Catherine Kelly. In Troy Mr. Kelly has always made his home. He received his education at the Christian Brothers' Academy and at the Troy High School. In the latter institution he was a student for two years and a half. Mr. Kelly is one of the best stenographers in the country, and for several years has been doing the Court reporting in Rensselaer, Columbia and the other counties of this judicial district. He has been doing stenographic work since 1882, and officially since Jan. 1, 1888. Mr. Kelly is also a practicing lawyer. He is the official stenographer of the Rensselaer County Court, having been appointed by Judge Fursman, and is also the official stenographer of the Columbia County Court, under the appointment of Judge McClellan. He is a member of the Bachelors' Club, the W. S. Earl Boat Club, and the J. C. Osgood Steamer Company. Mr. Kelly has the distinction of having been appointed stenographer of the Columbia County Court when he was only 21 years old, making him the youngest official stenographer in the State of New York.

Edward J. McKenna.

Edward J. McKenna.

EDWARD J. McKENNA was born in this city March 10, 1852. His parents were John and Elizabeth McKenna. He has always lived in Troy. Mr. McKenna was educated by the Christian Brothers and at the Second Ward public school. He started in life as a dry goods clerk, but later secured an appointment on the Troy police as a detective. He was promoted to police captain and is now in charge of the Third Precinct, having been in police service for fourteen years. He is a member and a trustee of the Hugh Ranken Steamer Company, and has been county sealer of weights and measures and a trustee of the Exempt Firemen's Association.

Walter A. Myers.

Walter A. Myers.

WALTER A. MYERS was born Nov. 1, 1852, in this city. His parents were Michael and Catherine Myers, and he has always resided in this city. He obtained his education in the public schools, and from 1868 to 1872 worked at the molder's trade. In 1879, '80 and '81 he was connected with the State Survey. In 1881 he was elected a general assessor for the term of three years, and later was made captain of police. He is now in charge of the First Precinct. Captain Myers represented the Ninth Ward in the Common Council from 1874 to 1880, and was recognized as one of the most energetic and conscientious of our city fathers. He was married Jan. 1, 1876, to Miss Jennie Hefferman, and has one child, a son 12 years old.

John Francis Ahern.

John Francis Ahern.

JOHN F. AHERN was born in this city March 1, 1850, the eldest son of Michael Ahern and Margaret Duffy. Mr. Ahern attended the public and the Christian Brothers' Schools and for four years was an assiduous student at Fordham College. His first work was as clerk of his father's hotel, the Union House. In 1873 he engaged in the retail liquor business on Third Street, the old "Crystal." Later he was for two years a clerk in the office of the Secretary of State, at Albany. He was a deputy sheriff under Sheriff Ingram. In 1882, associated with William Holmes, he opened a retail liquor establishment, and the firm are still in business at No. 12 Third Street. Mr. Ahern is treasurer of the Pilsner Democratic Club, a member of the Y. M. C. L. A. and the Bachelors' Club. He is also president of the Municipal Civil Service Board. He has been an alternate to several Democratic State conventions, and a ward committeeman for many years. He acted as treasurer of the committee which entertained Tammany Hall in this city in 1888. Mr. Ahern is married, his wife being Miss Julia F. Hickey.

William Henry Ryan.

William Henry Ryan.

WILLIAM H. RYAN was born in the city of New York March 9, 1856. His parents were Thomas and Margaret Ryan. When Mr. Ryan was four years of age his family removed to this city, and here he has remained ever since. He was educated in the public schools. For five years Mr. Ryan held a responsible position in the *Troy Times* office, and for ten years he was book-keeper for G. V. S. Quackenbush & Co., dry goods dealers. The past three years he has been book-keeper in the *Troy Press* office. He was manager of the paper when Edward Murphy, Jr., was in control of that property, and at the present time Mr. Ryan is vice-president and secretary of the *Press* Company. He is a thoroughly equipped newspaper man, and is one of the best accountants in the State.

John Quigley.

John Quigley.

JOHN QUIGLEY was born July 1, 1842, on board the sailing vessel "Niles," Captain Kenny, of Portland, Me. The ship was being flagged for the approaching Fourth of July when Mr. Quigley came into the world to greet the 120 passengers on the good ship "Niles." He was three weeks old when the vessel landed at New York, July 22, having occupied seven weeks in the passage over. Mr. Quigley's parents were Michael Quigley and Mary Collins. After remaining in New York they came to Troy, and here Mr. Quigley has since resided. He was educated in the public schools. For two years he was captain of police in the First Precinct, for four years captain in the Second Precinct, and for two years and six months superintendent of the Troy Police Force. From 1877 to 1880 he was a deputy sheriff. He was in command of the Pinkerton force on the Sheepshead Bay race track for two years, and for one year he did police duty in Canada. At present he is superintendent of streets. He is a member of the Robert Emmet Association and an honorary member of the Molders' Union, which trade he learned and worked at for several years. His wife's maiden name was Mary Collins. They have eight children, five boys and three girls. It was during Superintendent Quigley's administration that "Sheeny Mike" was caught and ex-Chamberlain Church arrested.

Alexander G. Cunningham.

Alexander G. Cunningham.

ALEXANDER G. CUNNINGHAM was born in Quebec May 2, 1855. His parents were Donald and Ellen Cunningham. When in his fourth year he was taken with his family to Montreal, where he lived six years. The past twenty-three years Mr. Cunningham has resided in Troy. After attending the Christian Brothers' Academy for several years he entered the employ of William Collins, sash and blind manufacturer, and remained with him as salesman until Mr. Collins sold out to Mann & Dater. On April 5, 1886, Mr. Cunningham formed a copartnership with J. L. Young, James R. Walsh and James T. Young, and the firm, under the name of Cunningham, Young & Co., have since been engaged in the manufacture of doors and blinds. They have a very large factory in West Troy. In 1879 and '80 Mr. Cunningham was vice-president of the Y. M. C. L. A. He is a member of the Edward Murphy, Jr., Association, the Y. M. C. L. A., the Robert Emmet Association and the Citizens' Corps. He was married Jan. 20, 1881, to Miss Mary A. Tracey.

Michael F. Ryan.

Michael F. Ryan.

MICHAEL F. RYAN, son of Michael and Mary Ryan, was born in this city Jan. 4, 1856. His education was obtained under the direction of the Christian Brothers. For ten years he worked at the shoemaking trade, and for seven years was a clerk in Bryan & Nugent's shoe store. In 1887 he was elected clerk of the Board of School Commissioners, succeeding the late Thomas W. Ryan, and has been twice reëlected. He is a member of the Robert Emmet Association and the Bachelors' Club. Mr. Ryan's wife, Miss Theresa Collins, is a sister of Supervisor Collins of the Tenth Ward.

James T. Murray.

James T. Murray.

JAMES T. MURRAY is the son of Martin and Ellen Murray, and was born in Rosscommon, Ireland, April 9, 1859. He has lived in Troy since 1862. Mr. Murray received his education in the public schools, the Christian Brothers' Academy and the High School, and was well equipped for the earnest work of life. After working as book-keeper for M. M. Willson, wholesale druggist, and Giles & Son, stove manufacturers, Mr. Murray accepted the position of principal of the Ninth Ward School, No. 2, where he remained three years. Meanwhile he had studied law. In 1881 he was admitted to the bar, and since has devoted all his time to his profession. Among the positions which Mr. Murray has filled are the following: President of the Debating Society of the Y. M. A., manager of the Y. M. C. L. A. and attorney for the Board of Supervisors in 1881, '82 and '83. He is a member of the Bachelors' Club and the Y. M. C. L. A. Mr. Murray studied law in the office of Smith, Fursman & Cowen.

James T. Quinn.

James T. Quinn.

JAMES T. QUINN was born in this city in 1855. His parents were Michael and Esther Quinn. He has always lived in Troy. After a course at the Christian Brothers' Academy, Mr. Quinn learned the carpenter's trade, at which he worked for twelve years. He is now in the liquor business. When Postmaster Dolan retired from the Common Council Mr. Quinn was elected to succeed him, representing the Eleventh Ward. He is a member of the Pilsner Democratic Club, the Edward Dolan Association and the Liquor Dealers' Association. Mr. Quinn has been signally successful both in business and political life.

Cornelius M. Dorsey.

Cornelius M. Dorsey.

CORNELIUS M. DORSEY first saw the light of day April 9, 1853, in London, England. His parents were James and Catherine Dorsey. He came to Troy in June, 1864. His family removed to Saratoga, but a year later came back to Troy. Mr. Dorsey's education was obtained in the public schools and at the Christian Brothers' Academy. At the age of sixteen he went to learn the painter's trade, and with the exception of four years, when he was employed at the Rensselaer Rail Mill, has worked at it ever since. He formed a copartnership, in 1883, with Daniel T. Holland, and the firm of Holland & Dorsey are now doing business at No. 195 Fourth Street. Mr. Dorsey was a prominent member of the Y. M. F. M. T. A. B. Society, No. 1, and held the offices of president and secretary at different times. He is a member of the C. B. L., Branch 66, the Y. M. C. L. A. and the Edward Murphy, Jr., Association. He is married, his wife being Miss Mary Moylan.

William Hutton, Jr.

William Hutton, Jr.

WILLIAM HUTTON, JR., was born in this city Sept. 1, 1863, his parents being William Hutton and Bridget McGowan. Mr. Hutton has always made his home in Troy. After graduating from the Christian Brothers' Academy he entered the employ of E. W. Millard, the undertaker, where he remained one year. Later he was in the employ of John McBride, but the past four years the subject of this sketch has b en his father's book-keeper. Mr. Hutton is a member of the Y. M. C. L. A., Christian Brothers' Alumni and the Bachelors' Club. He was married Nov. 28, 1888, to Miss Carrie, the accomplished daughter of William Kennedy, our much respected townsman.

Mark J. Coyle.

Mark J. Coyle.

MARK J. COYLE was born in Quincy. Mass., Sept. 1, 1863. His parents were Mark J. and Mary A. Coyle. At the age of seven Mark removed with his parents to Albany, where he lived four years. The past fourteen years he has resided in Troy. Mr. Coyle received his education in the public schools of Quincy, Mass., and Albany, N. Y. When a mere lad he entered the employ of Daniel Walters, the Albany oyster dealer, and came to Troy with Mr. Walters when the latter removed his business to this city. In 1882 Mr. Coyle bought out Mr. Walters' stand at No. 90 Third Street. In May, 1888, he removed to No. 69 Third Street, opposite the City Hall, where he is at present located. Mr. Coyle is a prominent member of the Edward Murphy, Jr., Association, of which he held the office of treasurer. He is now one of the trustees. He is also a member of the Bachelors' Club, the Y. M. C. L. A. and the Liquor Dealers' Association. Few young men in this or any other city have done so much for their parents and those dependent upon them as has Mark J. Coyle, and his success in business has been most gratifying to his host of friends.

Michael Grace.

Michael Grace.

MICHAEL GRACE, son of John and Ellen Grace, was born in this city April 10, 1849. In Troy he has always made his home. After obtaining a sound education at St. Joseph's School he began his apprenticeship at the molding trade in 1867, and followed it until 1877, when he was appointed a patrolman on the Troy Police Force. He was promoted to the post of sergeant in 1881, and was reappointed in November, 1885. Sergeant Grace is assigned to the First Precinct. The only organizations of which he has been a member are the Molders' Union and Y. M. F. M. T. A. B. Society, No. 1. He has an enviable record on the police force, and is popular and respected.

Daniel A. Healy.

Daniel A. Healy.

DANIEL A. HEALY was born in this city twenty-three years ago. He is the son of Martin Healy. After a thorough course in the public schools he determined to learn the druggist's business, and for several years he was in the employ of Joseph Donnelly, at the corner of Adams and Second Streets, acting as prescription clerk. He passed a brilliant examination as a pharmacist. August 1, 1887, Mr. Healy went into business for himself at No. 506 Second Street, and a few months ago, associated with his brother, John, he opened a branch establishment at No. 223 Fourth Street, under the firm name of J. J. Healy & Co. Daniel Healy has been collector of Iron Works Council, C. B. L., since its organization.

James J. Duffy.

James J. Duffy.

JAMES J. DUFFY, son of James Duffy and Ellen McEncrow, was born in this city December 25, 1855. With the exception of four years, ending 1876, when he resided in St. Louis, Mr. Duffy has always resided in Troy. He was educated at the Christian Brothers' Academy. For four years he was agent for Coleman Bros., the Albany brewers. At present he is in the wholesale liquor business in this city. He is a member of the Pilsner Club, the W. S. Earl Boat Club, the A. O. H., the Emeralds, and Olympic Council, C. B. L. Mr. Duffy is married, his wife being Miss Jennie McEntire, of Brooklyn. They have three children, Nellie, aged 8; James, aged 6, and Mary, aged 4 years.

John J. Purcell.

John J. Purcell.

JOHN J. PURCELL was born in Ireland March 22, 1858, while his parents, John C. Purcell and Johanna Williams, were on a visit to the old country. He was two months old when he first breathed the air of free America. He obtained his education in the Christian Brothers' School, the public schools and at the High School, and learned the plumbing trade from the late John E. Smith, of Nos. 5 and 7 State Street. Mr. Purcell started in business for himself in 1882, at No. 412 Second Street, and is now associated with his brother, Thomas B. Purcell. He is in the plumbing, gas and steam fitting trade at Nos. 411 and 413 Second Street. In 1883 he was elected a member of the Common Council from the Twelfth Ward, and he is still a member of the Board. For three years he was a manager of the Y. M. C. L. A. and for three years he was treasurer of the organization. He is a member of the Y. M. C. L. A., Emeralds, Branch 6, and the A. O. H., No. 1. Mr. Purcell was married Nov. 2, 1888, to Miss Annie F. Donovan.

William H. Haynes.

William H. Haynes.

WILLIAM H. HAYNES, son of Winslow Haynes and Catherine Pillion, was born in this city in 1851, and has lived here all his life. He was educated in the public schools and the Christian Brothers' Academy. Upon leaving school he determined to learn the trade of a carpenter. He served his apprenticeship with George W. Oliver, and then formed a copartnership with John Bulmer, under the firm name of Bulmer & Haynes, contractors and builders. These gentlemen have been very successful in their business. Mr. Haynes served as president of the Boss Builders' Association for three successive terms. He is a member of this association and of the Edward Dolan Association. Mr. Haynes' estimable wife, Miss Lizzie Bulmer, to whom he was married Oct. 12, 1878, died Jan. 23, 1889.

Edward A. Lovelock.

Edward A. Lovelock.

EDWARD A. LOVELOCK was born August 19, 1862, at Sheffield, Mass., the son of Patrick and Kate Lovelock. During his early years Mr. Lovelock's parents resided in Half Moon, Saratoga County, West Troy and Brunswick, but the greater part of his life has been spent in this city. He attended the country schools, and, later, worked in the rolling mill, at the cigar business and at farming. At present he is in the retail liquor trade. He has been captain and trustee of the W. S. Earl Boat Club, and is now a member of the Board of Managers of the Y. M. C. L. A.` He is also a member of the Washington Volunteer Steamer Company and the United States Coasting Club. In business Mr. Lovelock has been very successful.

Daniel T. Holland.

Daniel T. Holland.

DANIEL T. HOLLAND was born Nov. 4, 1853, at Scranton, Pa. He was the son of Stephen and Ellen Holland. The family came to Troy March 4, 1857. Mr. Holland was educated at the Christian Brothers' Academy and the Bryant, Stratton & Cornell Business College. When quite young Mr. Holland kept newsrooms at No. 299 Fourth Street and at No. 90 Congress Street. He went into business later on with his father, a dealer in picture frames, etc., but in 1870 sold out and began an apprenticeship at the painter's trade with the late John McKanna. He has followed that trade ever since. At present he is associated with C. M. Dorsey, under the firm name of Holland & Dorsey, and they are doing a general painting business. For fifteen years Mr. Holland has been a member of the Y. M. F. M. T. A. B. Society, No. 1, during which time he has held every office in the organization. He is secretary of the Master Painters' and Decorators' Association, and is also secretary of the State organization of his craft. He is a member of the Edward Murphy, Jr., Association, and of the C. B. L., Branch No. 66, of which he is a trustee. He was married Sept. 8, 1878, to Miss Mary J. Farley, and has one child, a daughter, eight years old.

James W. Daly.

James W. Daly.

JAMES W. DALY was born in this city Dec. 14, 1857. His parents were James and Ellen Daly. Mr. Daly attended the public schools, and quite early in life entered the office of Christie & Boardman, insurance agents. Later he was a drug clerk in the wholesale house of Robinson & Church. Mr. Daly subsequently served as book-keeper in the establishment of Holland & Thompson. When that firm retired from the city Mr. Daly became associated with Messrs. Chamberlain and Bottum, who successfully carried on the business. Last year the firm was dissolved and Mr. Daly is now associated with Mr. Bottum, and is conducting a large steam, gas and plumbers' supplies store. He was elected Alderman from the Eleventh Ward in 1886 and was reëlected in 1888. Mr. Daly took a prominent part in arranging Troy's centennial celebration, and to his efforts much of the success of the affair is due. Although still a very young man Mr. Daly has made his mark in the business world.

Thomas D. Hendy.

Thomas D. Hendy.

THOMAS D. HENDY was born May 14, 1862, in this city, at the corner of Ida and First Streets, and there he still resides. His parents were Daniel and Margaret Hendy. Mr. Hendy was educated at the Christian Brothers' Academy. For twelve years he was a clerk. He is now in the liquor business. He has served as manager of the Y. M. C. L. A. and as secretary of the Debating Society. He is a member of the Board of School Commissioners, and is probably the youngest man who ever sat with that important city commission. He is also a member of the Democratic County Committee, the Pilsner Democratic Club and the Osgood Steamer Company. He was married to Miss Lizzie C. Davis Jan. 3, 1881. She died July 18, 1888.

Samuel Edward Hutton.

Samuel Edward Hutton.

THE SUBJECT of this sketch is the eldest son of William Hutton and Bridget McGowan. He was born in this city June 25, 1855. With the exception of the interval between 1876 and 1881, when Mr. Hutton resided in New York, he has always made Troy his home. He secured his education at the Christian Brothers' Academy. After leaving school he worked for three years in the foundry of William P. Kellogg & Co. Then he entered his father's employ as book-keeper and general manager of his large livery establishment. Until recently, when he retired, Mr. Hutton was the senior member of the firm of Hutton & Fennell, cigar manufacturers. The only political office he has ever held was that of Registrar of Vital Statistics, from May 1885, to May, 1888. At present he is president of the Debating Society of the Y. M. C. L. A., trustee of the F. W. Farnam Steamer Company and recording secretary of the Edward Murphy, Jr., Association. He is also a member of the Bachelors' Club, Emerald Beneficial Association, Branch 6, and Alumni Association of the Christian Brothers' Academy. Mr. Hutton's wife was Miss Frances V. McCormick.

Henry A. Conway.

Henry A. Conway.

HENRY A. CONWAY was born in this city August 8, 1859, the son of John and Mary Conway. He was educated at St. Peter's Parochial School, and then entered the employ of John Skellie, retail liquor dealer, at No. 6 State Street. Five years later Mr. Conway succeeded to the business. He has never held political position, his taste not running in that direction. He is a member of the Robert Emmet Association, the Bachelors' Club and the Y. M. C. L. A. A few years ago Mr. Conway sold out his State Street business to his brother, William, and associating himself with his brother, Daniel E., and the late Congressman Nicholas T. Kane, purchased the old Sands brewery property on North Fourth Street, and has since been engaged in the brewing of ales and porters. The firm of Conway Bros. & Kane rates high and is considered one of the leading brewing concerns of the country. Mr. Conway's wife was Miss Teresa Healey, the accomplished niece of the late Congressman Kane. Mr. and Mrs. Conway have one child, a boy.

Henry Joseph McCormick.

Henry Joseph McCormick.

HENRY J. McCORMICK is the eldest son of John and Catherine McCormick. He was born in West Troy Sept. 28, 1864. His parents removed to this city in 1870. Until twelve years of age Henry attended the public schools. Then he entered the Brothers' Academy, and in 1884 he graduated with high honors from that institution. Immediately after leaving school he began the study of law in the office of Robertson & Foster, and in September, 1887, was admitted to the bar. He enjoys a flattering practice, and is recognized as an able and worthy young practitioner. He is a member of the Y. M. C. L. A. and the Earl Boat Club.

John P. Prendergast.

John P. Prendergast.

JOHN P. PRENDERGAST was born in Manchester, England, March 2, 1853, the son of Patrick and Catherine Prendergast. For three years he resided in New York, but since January, 1859, he has lived in this city. He obtained his education at the Christian Brothers' Academy and the Albany Medical College. From 1870 until 1873 he served in Company B, Sixth U. S. Cavalry, U. S. A. Upon graduating from the Albany Medical College he began to practice in this city, and his success as a physician and surgeon has been marked. He was city physician in 1880, and in 1884, '86, '87 and '89 was jail physician. He is a member of the Hugh Ranken Steamer Company, the E. B. A., Branch 3, and Mount Olympus Council, No. 142, C. B. L. He was married June 22, 1881, to Miss Catherine Griffin.

Patrick J. Delaney.

Patrick J. Delaney.

PATRICK J. DELANEY was born in Ireland July 4, 1863. His parents were Martin Delaney and Julia Tracey. When he was an infant, the Delaney family came to Troy, and here the subject of this sketch has since resided. He was educated by the Christian Brothers and then entered the employ of the Burdett & Smith Co., stove manufacturers, as book-keeper, where he has since remained. He represents the Twelfth Ward in the Common Council, and has frequently acted as chairman of that body. He is a member of the J. C. Osgood Steamer Company, the Robert Emmet Association and the Bachelors' Club. For so young a man, Alderman Delaney has attained a remarkable prominence in the community.

Thomas B. Purcell.

Thomas B. Purcell.

THOMAS B. PURCELL was born in this city May 24, 1856, his parents being John C. Purcell and Johanna Williams. He was educated by the Christian Brothers, and then learned the trade of a tinsmith from Michael Doherty, of No. 521 Fourth Street. In 1876 Mr. Purcell went into business for himself and from the very beginning was successful. His present place of business is at Nos. 411 and 413 Second Street. In 1887 he was elected a member of the Board of Fire Commissioners and he is still a member of that Board. He is president of A. O. H., No. 1, president of the J. C. Osgood Steamer Company, and was president of the Y. M. F. M. T. A. B. Society, No. 1. In 1885 and '86 he was Rensselaer County delegate of the A. O. H. He was married May 21, 1882, to Miss Margaret E. Crossen, and has two children, daughters, aged six and two years.

Joseph Henry Cavanaugh.

Joseph Henry Cavanaugh.

JOSEPH H. CAVANAUGH was born March 27, 1859, in this city. His parents were Patrick and Emma Cavanaugh, and in this city he has always made his home. He was educated at the Fourth Ward public school. His first work was done in J. G. Bacon & Son's insurance office. Later he was clerk for Judge & Cavanaugh, contractors, and learned the trade of a mason. He is now a contractor and builder, and has constructed many public works of great magnitude. Mr. Cavanaugh represented the Fourth Ward in the Common Council for one term. He is a member of the Pilsner Club, is married and has one child, a little girl. His wife's maiden name was Maggie E. Purcell.

Con. F. Burns.

Con. F. Burns.

Con. F. Burns, son of John W. and Ellen Burns, was born in this city Nov. 4, 1860. His father was Troy's leading undertaker and all of his sons were given the best educational advantages. Con. graduated with high honors from the Christian Brothers' Academy, and immediately thereafter entered his father's office. John W. Burns died April 9, 1880, and to his business succeeded his sons, George and Con. F. Two years later George died and at present the subject of this sketch is at the head of the firm of J. W. Burns' Sons, his associates being his brothers, James and David. Con. is a member of the Bachelors' and Pilsner Clubs, the Y. M. C. L. A., Trojan Hooks, Exempt Firemen's Association, Undertakers' Association of the State (of which for two years he has been treasurer) and the local association of undertakers, of which he is president. Mr. Burns is the president of the Bachelors' Club and has served as vice-president and secretary of the organization. He is chairman of the Board of Trustees of the Pilsner Club. For two years he has been president of the St. Vincent Female Orphan Asylum fair. Last year, under the direction of Mr. Burns, the fair netted $8,000, marking it as the most successful enterprise of the kind ever held in Troy. Mr. Burns acted as grand marshal of the monster Democratic parade in this city in the fall of 1888.

George E. Sands.

George E. Sands.

GEORGE E. SANDS was born in this city March 10, 1861, his parents being Daniel E. Sands and Ellen Madigan. George was educated in the public schools, graduating with honors from the High School in 1879. After serving as book-keeper in Kennedy & Murphy's brewing establishment, Mr. Sands accepted the position of principal of Ninth Ward School, No. 2, where he remained until the discontinuance of the school. Subsequently he held reportorial and editorial positions on the Troy *Standard, Telegram, Budget* and *Press,* and the Albany *Sunday Telegram,* of which he was the local business manager for Troy and the correspondent. Mr. Sands abandoned journalism to accept a post of great responsibility in the city comptroller's office, succeeding George H. Coon. He has been president of the Debating Society of the Y. M. C. L. A., and is a member of the William S. Earl Boat Club, Y. M. C. L. A. and the Pilsner Democratic Club.

Edward L. Lyons.

Edward L. Lyons.

EDWARD L. LYONS was born in this city January 29, 1863, his parents being Edward and Ellen Lyons. He attended the Brothers' Academy until 1879 when he removed to New York. He graduated with high honors from the New York University Medical College after six years of hard and persistent study. In order to round out his medical education Dr. Lyons visited Europe, where he devoted a year to study and research, the most of the time being spent in Berlin and Vienna. Dr. Lyons returned to Troy in October, 1888, and immediately attained success in the practice of his sublime profession. Dr. Lyons is recognized as one of the most promising of our younger generation of practitioners. He is a member of the C. B. L. and A. O. H., No. 2.

Charles H. F. Cary.

Charles H. F. Cary.

CHARLES H. F. CARY, son of James and Mary Cary, was born in this city Feb. 6, 1866, in the house No. 19 Hill Street. Mr. Cary has always lived in Troy. At the Christian Brothers' Academy he received a splendid education. April 29, 1886, he was admitted to partnership with his father in the undertaking business. Their warerooms are located at No. 227 Fourth Street. While in no way abandoning his interest in the undertaking business, Mr. Cary embarked in the retail boot and shoe trade at No. 231 Fourth Street on July 29, 1889. In both his business ventures Mr. Cary has achieved conspicuous success. He is a member of the Edward Murphy, Jr., Association, and is the marshal of that organization. On February 11, 1889, he was married to Miss Kittie Welch, an accomplished young lady, who has been to him a wise counselor and conservative guide.

James P. Hooley.

James P. Hooley.

JAMES P. Hooley was born of Irish parents July 12, 1855, in Port Chester, Conn. He came from New York to Troy in 1865. He attended St. Peter's School until he was twelve years old, and then he entered a public school, where he remained two years. He was apprenticed to learn the trade of a molder at the age of seventeen, and after serving four years was admitted to membership in the Iron Molders' Union. In 1882 he was chosen a delegate to the International Molders' Convention held in Brooklyn. He was elected third vice-president. Thereafter he became actively engaged in the work of organizing labor societies. He was chairman of the organizing committee of the Workingmen's Assembly, and was three times elected organizer of the Knights of Labor. Mr. Hooley personally investigated the contract labor system in the State prisons. In the fall of 1884 he was elected to the Assembly from the First District of Rensselaer County. During the session of the Legislature which followed contract prison labor was abolished, Mr. Hooley having charge of this most important reform in the Assembly. He was reëlected to the Assembly in 1885, but was defeated for a third term. In 1886 he attended the convention of the International Iron Molders' Union held in London, Canada, and was reëlected a member of the Executive Board and of the Board of Trustees. In June, 1887, he was appointed a factory inspector. The following year he was chosen vice-president of the International Iron Molders' Union of North America at the Convention held in St. Louis. Mr. Hooley is an accomplished musician, having been a member of Doring's Band since 1876. Mr. Hooley's career in politics was one long and determined effort to improve the condition of the working classes, and the measure of success he attained gave him a reputation wider than the State in which he labored.

Michael P. Flaherty.

Michael P. Flaherty.

MICHAEL P. FLAHERTY was born in the First Ward of the city of Troy January 14, 1850. His parents were John Flaherty and Mary Heffernan, both natives of Ireland. With the exception of a few years, when he resided in New York, the subject of this sketch has made his home in this city. He was educated in the Christian Brothers' Academy. He enlisted as a volunteer in the Ninety-first New York Regiment, and has the distinction of having been one of the youngest of the patriotic boys who went to the front when the life of the nation was threatened. For seventeen years he was employed as a time-keeper in the Rensselaer Iron Works. He is at present engaged in the drug and grocery trade, and has a very large and constantly increasing business. Among the offices which Mr. Flaherty has filled were prefect of the Young Men's Sodality of St. Joseph's Church and president of the Five Points' Guards. He is a member of the Edward Murphy, Jr., Association, the I. D. K. Association, the Y. M. C. L. A., the Osgood Steamer Company and the Five Points' Guards. Mr. Flaherty is married, his wife's maiden name being Johanna M. Regan. They have two children, a boy of sixteen and a girl of thirteen.

Michael H. Keating.

Michael H. Keating.

MICHAEL H. KEATING was born March 31, 1860, in this city. He is the son of John Keating and Mary Nutley, and has always lived in Troy. He secured his education at the Sixth Ward Public School. For twelve years he was hydraulic engineer at the steel works. Mr. Keating was engaged for a year in the retail liquor business on River Street, but several months ago he retired from the trade. He represents the Sixth Ward in the Common Council, and is recognized as one of the ablest members of that body. Mr. Keating is young and energetic and his future is full of the ripest promise.

John J. Hartigan.

John J. Hartigan.

JOHN J. HARTIGAN was born in this city October 31, 1853. His parents were Maurice and Ellen Hartigan, the latter recently deceased. It was at the Christian Brothers' Academy that Mr. Hartigan obtained his splendid education. Upon completing the course at the Academy he entered the dry goods store of George Bristol & Co. He remained with the succeeding firms, Church & Phalen and the Andrew M. Church Company, until November 24, 1888, when he began business for himself on King Street, ten doors below Jacob Street, where he has already established a large dry goods trade. Mr. Hartigan was vice-president of the Robert Emmet Association in 1887, and was president of the same organization in 1888 and 1889. In 1888 he was chosen vice-president of the Alumni Association of the Christian Brothers' Academy. For ten years, from 1875 to 1885, he was a director of the Apollo Vocal Society. He is a member of the Robert Emmet Association, the Y. M. C. L. A. and the Troy Vocal Society. Mr. Hartigan's wife was Miss Libbie Clogan. To unflagging industry and a genius for the business to which he has devoted his life is due Mr. Hartigan's mercantile success.

Thomas S. Fagan.

Thomas S. Fagan.

THOMAS S. FAGAN was born in this city January 18, 1862. He is the son of Michael G. and Catherine Fagan. Mr. Fagan attended the public schools and in 1878 graduated from the High School with the highest honors, being the class valedictorian. He immediately entered Williams College, from which he was graduated in 1882. He took the prize for having taken the greatest number of prizes, a remarkable distinction for the young student. For two years he acted as tutor and assistant principal of the High School in Troy. He studied law during his leisure time, and in 1885 was admitted to the bar. Two years later he was elected a justice of the Justices' Court of the city of Troy, serving one term. He is a member of the Phi Beta-Kappa, having been elected a member of the Williams College Chapter in 1881 for excellence in scholarship. In 1881 he was selected by the students of the college to receive President Carter on his inauguration as president of the college. He is a lawyer of rare attainments and large practice. As a public speaker, Mr. Fagan ranks high among the younger generation of lawyers in this State.

William T. Shields.

William T. Shields.

WILLIAM T. SHIELDS was born July 19, 1863, in Jackson, Washington County, N. Y. He is the son of John Shields and Ellen O'Brien. He attended the public schools and the Christian Brothers' Academy, and then learned the trade of telegraph operator. He left Troy in 1881 and went to Chicago, where he resided for some time, going thence to St. Louis, where he worked as a telegrapher for eighteen months. Later he was employed in New York. In 1884 he returned to Troy and for a year received the United Press report in the office of the *Standard*. After filling responsible positions in New York he accepted on October 9, 1887, the position of Associated Press operator on the *Telegram*, where for two years he did remarkably fine work which stamped him as one of the best operators in the country. He was one of the charter members of the Brotherhood of Telegraphers in St. Louis and was its financial secretary. He is married, his wife's maiden name being Margaret C. O'Connor. They have two children, both boys.

James H. Ryan.

James H. Ryan.

JAMES H. RYAN was born on Fourth Street, this city, February 20, 1856, the son of Daniel and Honora Ryan. After a preliminary course in the Christian Brothers' Academy Mr. Ryan attended Manhattan Academy, Manhattan College, and Rock Hill College, Ellicott City, Md. He received a finished education, and then studied law in the office of H. A. Merritt. Immediately after his admission to the bar he sprang into prominence as a pleader, and to-day has few equals in this part of the State in criminal practice. As the junior member of the firm of Merritt & Ryan he is well and favorably known in this section. He has served as attorney for the village of Greenbush, and this year is the attorney for the Board of Supervisors of Rensselaer County. He is a member of the Bachelors' Club. Mr. Ryan's wife was Miss Ellen McNamara. They have two beautiful children, Mary, aged 5, and Florence, aged 3.

John E. Healey.

John E. Healey.

JOHN E. HEALEY, one of Troy's leading wholesale merchants, was born thirty-four years ago, in West Troy, of Irish parents. He was educated in the public schools and the schools of the Christian Brothers. Mr. Healey entered upon his business career, embarking in the wholesale produce and commission business in the store No. 191 River St., corner of State, in March, 1873. After using that location until the spring of 1878, he moved farther up-town with the drift of trade, which was steadily going north of Fulton Market, and is now located in the store No. 333 River St., which he has adapted to his business by erecting an elaborate system of refrigerators in the rear, on Mechanic St. end of the building, this being a necessity to meet largely increased trade requirements. His specialties are butter, cheese and eggs. He was one of the first dealers north of New York to adopt the use of refrigerator cars, and was the pioneer receiver of the products of the North-West for this section. Mr. Healey filled the position of school trustee for the Third Ward, West Troy, for nine years, from 1876 to 1885. He is married and has four interesting children, two boys and two girls. In his career Mr. Healey has exhibited what can be accomplished by strict integrity and a close application to the demands of business. He has been remarkably successful, being well and favorably known throughout the West and North-West, and possesses the confidence of all the merchants of Troy.

John H. Flaherty.

John H. Flaherty.

JOHN H. FLAHERTY was born in Troy July 23, 1863, and here he has always lived. His parents were William H. and Margaret Flaherty. In the Sisters' School, the Thirteenth Ward Public School and the Troy Business College Mr. Flaherty secured his education. For several years he worked in markets and grocery stores, striving to master the business. That he was successful is evidenced by the fact that to-day he is the proprietor of a large grocery store which enjoys a very profitable trade. For five consecutive years he was the treasurer of the E. B. A., No. 3. He has also served as president of the Y. M. C. L. A. and the Hugh Ranken Steamer Company. He is a member of the executive board of the G. B., E. B. A., of the State of New York, a member of the Grocers' and Butchers' Association, E. B. A., No. 3, Hugh Ranken Steamer Company and the Esek Bussey Hose Company. Mr. Flaherty stands high in this community, and his future is all that his friends could wish for him.

Joseph H. Broderick.

Joseph H. Broderick.

JOSEPH H. BRODERICK was born Sept. 11, 1855, in this city. He is the son of Michael and Hannah Broderick. After a public school course Mr. Broderick learned the trade of boiler maker, at which he worked for sixteen years. In 1884 he began the manufacture of cigars, and in that business he has attained a flattering success. He is a member of the Bachelors' Club and the Catholic Benevolent Legion. Mr. Broderick's wife, Miss Mary Conway, died Sept. 13, 1888. He has one child, a boy. Mr. Broderick is essentially a business man. His social position is high, and his future is bright with promise.

Michael J. Duffy.

Michael J. Duffy.

MICHAEL J. DUFFY was born in this city February 17, 1862, the son of James and Ellen Duffy. He has always made his home in this city. For several years he was a student in St. Laurent College, Montreal, and there he was graduated and received a splendid education. Few young men are so fortunate in their educational advantages. After leaving school he was employed for seven years as a bookkeeper. At present he is in the real estate and insurance business. In 1888 he was president of the Y. M. C. L. A. He is a member of the Earl Boat Club and the Washington Volunteer Steamer Company. From 1885 to 1888 he was the secretary of the Earl Boat Club.

Ambrose Kelly.

Ambrose Kelly.

THERE is no better known business man in Troy than the subject of this sketch. He was born in this city January 30, 1855. His parents were James and Mary A. Kelly. Mr. Kelly was educated at the Christian Brothers' Academy, and was, of course, thoroughly prepared for the work of a business man. Upon leaving school, in 1869, Mr. Kelly entered the employ of the late James Dennin, the grocer, and remained until Mr. Dennin's death in 1882. For the succeeding two years Mr. Kelly conducted the business for the estate of Mr. Dennin, and then he purchased the business which he has made the best known grocery stand in Troy. In 1875-6 Mr. Kelly was the secretary of the Y. M. C. L. A. He was a charter member and the first president of Mount Ida Council, C. B. L. He is also orator of the State Council, C. B. L., and district deputy state chancellor. He is a member of the Robert Emmet Association, the Bachelors' Club and of several musical organizations. Mr. Kelly was married in 1880 to Miss Mary Peters and has four children, two boys and two girls.

James C. Minahan.

James C. Minahan.

JAMES C. MINAHAN was born in this city August 21, 1857, the son of John and Mary Minahan. He was educated in the public schools. On October 3, 1869, he began work as a messenger boy in the office of the Western Union Company and speedily learned the trade of telegraph operator, at which he became remarkably expert. He managed the Baltimore & Ohio and Mutual Union offices in this city, and had the confidence of these great corporations. Among operators Mr. Minahan was recognized as one of the best in the country. He has made a special study of electrical science, and at present is assistant manager of the Troy Electric Light Company. He is a leading member of the Bachelors' Club. Mr. Minahan was married October 24, 1888, to Miss Margaret English, daughter of John English.

Bernard M. Roarke.

Bernard M. Roarke.

BERNARD M. ROARKE was born in Ireland December 19, 1843, the son of Patrick Roarke and Mary Malone. He has resided in Albany and Troy nearly all of his life. He attended the Brothers' Academy and the public schools. He first worked for Stevens & Rising, the Cannon Place Merchants, and later was in the employ of the Hudson River Railroad Company under Mr. Toucey, now the superintendent of the Central-Hudson. He worked also on the old Rensselaer & Saratoga Road, and afterward learned the trade of a brick-layer. He remained steadily at his trade until 1876 when he was appointed a detective on the police force. He did police duty until 1883, winning the highest encomiums from his superiors for his faithfulness. In 1883 he was chosen to represent the Eighth Ward in the Common Council, and so ably did he serve his constituents that he was reëlected in 1885 and in 1887. He declined a renomination last year. May 10, 1886, Alderman Roarke was appointed a custom-house officer and he served three years. He is at present in the retail liquor trade at the corner of Washington and Fourth Streets. He was married January 6, 1886, to Miss Catherine Halpin, and has two pretty and bright children. Bernard Roarke is one of the most popular men in Troy. He has innumerable friends who are as devoted to him as he is to them.

John H. Gleason.

John H. Gleason.

JOHN H. GLEASON, one of Troy's most popular citizens, was born in Schenectady, N. Y., September 25, 1844. He lived in "Old Dorp" until he was twelve years of age when he came to Troy and attended school for three years. At the expiration of this period he returned to Schenectady, but in his eighteenth year he decided to learn the trade of a blacksmith and came to Troy for that purpose. He served a thorough apprenticeship with Daniel Lucey and Culkin & Donohue. For the five following years he worked in the shops on Starbuck's Island. Then he went into the black-smithing business for himself at No. 124 Fourth Street where he remained five years, moving to the Dennin Building, at the foot of Fulton Street. He rented the ship-yard from the city and retained possession of it for six years. While he controlled this yard which has since disappeared, occurred the famous Gleason-Hancock war. The Hancock line of steamers insisted on landing at Mr. Gleason's dock and refused to recognize the fact that he was the tenant and the city the landlord. Mr. Gleason triumphed in the end, and the whole city was brought to admire his pluck and determination. When his lease of the ship-yard expired Mr. Gleason erected a brick shop at the foot of the street and remained there in business until two years ago, when he was appointed assistant superintendent of the water-works and keeper of the reservoirs. These positions he still holds, discharging their onerous and responsible duties with eminent satisfaction. For nine years Mr. Gleason was a member of the Board of School Commissioners. He refused an offer of the presidency of this commission. For one year, under Governor John T. Hoffman, he was inspector of steam boilers for this Congressional District. Mr. Gleason was a deputy sheriff for three years under Sheriff McKeon, for three years under Sheriff Hotchkin and for three years under Sheriff Reynolds. Mr. Gleason has been prominent for years in the councils of the Democratic party. He was a delegate to the Saratoga convention which two years ago re-nominated Governor David B. Hill. Mr. Gleason is a member of the Pilsners, the Edward Murphy, Jr., Association and the Exempt Firemen's Association. He is married, his wife having been Miss Margaret E. Inwood. Three children, John E., Robert I. and Mary Alice, are the light and the joy of the lives of Mr. and Mrs. Gleason. A daughter, who was a teacher in the public schools, died not long since.

William R. Sweeney.

William R. Sweeney.

WILLIAM R. SWEENEY was born in Tipperary, Ireland, in 1854, being the son of Edmund Sweeney and Winifred O'Donnell. Both of his parents are dead. Since boyhood the subject of this sketch has resided in Troy. He obtained a splendid education at the Christian Brothers' Academy of this city. From a small beginning Mr. Sweeney at present is the proprietor of one of the largest bakeries in the city. He employs twenty hands and has five delivery wagons on the road every day distributing the product of his immense bakery. In addition to this Mr. Sweeney is the wholesale agent for this section of the celebrated Kennedy Cracker Co. of Cambridgeport, Mass. He has been prefect of the Young Men's Sodality of St. Joseph's Church, president of St. Joseph's Literary Association, treasurer of the J. C. Osgood Steamer Company, and is at present a member of the Byron Literary Association, a member of the Executive Committee of the Citizens' Association, representing the Twelfth Ward in that body, on the Executive Committee of the Young Men's Democratic Club, a member of the Robert Emmet Association and a trustee of the Alumni Association of St. Mary's Academy. He is married, his wife being the daughter of the Hon. James Ryan, Jr., of this city. They have six children living and two dead. As an evidence of the esteem in which he is held in this community, Mr. Sweeney has recently been unanimously elected and is now acting as clerk of the new Public Improvement Commission.

John P. Powers.

John P. Powers.

JOHN PATRICK POWERS was born in Oneida, N. Y., July 22, 1855. His father was Patrick Powers and his mother Mary Dunlay. The Powers family moved to Troy twenty-one years ago and here John has ever since made his home. He was educated at the Brothers' Academy and was then apprenticed to learn the trade of a compositor in the office of the Troy *Press*. Having learned the trade he worked for a time on the *Standard*. Eleven years ago he quit the " case " and became book-keeper in the *Press* counting room. For three years he served as a clerk in the office of the State Board of Arbitration. For three years he was the efficient and enterprising manager of Rand's Opera House. He has been connected with a number of theatrical ventures. At present he is treasurer of the Griswold Opera House. He was a member of the Y. M. F. M. T. A. B. Society for twelve years. He is a member of the Edward Murphy, Jr., Association. Mr. Powers is married and has two bright children. His wife was Miss Mary McDonnell.

Thomas P. Dowling.

Thomas P. Dowling.

THOMAS P. DOWLING was born in this city December 28, 1854, the son of Edward Dowling, who was killed at the battle of Gettysburg July 4, 1863, and Anna Cassidy Langford. The parents of Mr. Dowling were natives of Ireland, but they were married in this city. In the public schools Mr. Dowling obtained his education. He began early to make his way in the world, and, like many other men who have attained prominence and high business standing in this community, delivered the daily and weekly papers over long and tiresome routes. He worked for Levi Willard and H. B. Nims, the stationers, and later, for seven years, was in the employ of the Granite Monument Works. In 1877 he entered the employ of E. F. Rogers, the Sixth Street laundryman, at a small salary. He quickly mastered the business and, upon the retirement of Mr. Rogers, became the proprietor of one of the best-known concerns of the kind in the country. The laundry turns out an immense amount of work, and is famed for its excellence all over the country. From 1885 to 1889 Mr. Dowling was a member of the Municipal Civil Service Board. In 1885 he was elected treasurer of the Board of Trustees of the Troy fire department, serving in that capacity until the present year. He is

a member of the Robert Emmet Association, the Bachelors'
Club and the Trojan Hooks. Mr. Dowling's wife is Miss
Mary F. Keenan, daughter of ex-Sheriff Keenan. They
have one child, a bright three-year-old boy. For so young a
man Mr. Dowling has achieved marvelous success. In his
life, boys who are struggling along to-day should find the
encouragement to lead them to persistent, honorable and
earnest endeavor.

Dennis J. Cummings.

Dennis J. Cummings.

DENNIS J. CUMMINGS was born in this city December 3, 1852, the son of Thomas and Mary Cummings. After attending the public schools until he had obtained a good education he was apprenticed to learn the trade of a carpenter, at which he worked for six years. For several years past he has been in the retail liquor trade, and has been very successful. Mr. Cummings has been prominent in politics, having served in the Board of Supervisors and as coroner of the county. He is a member of the William S. Earl Boat Club, the Pilsner Democratic Club and the I. D. K. Association. He was married June 13, 1876, to Miss Mary Duffy. They have three children, two girls and a boy. Mr. Cummings is well and favorably known in this section, and his popularity with all classes of people is marked. In 1870, through the influence of the late Hon. John L. Flagg, Mr. Cummings was appointed a page in the Assembly. The following year he joined the Washington Volunteer Steamer Company and later the Charles Eddy Steamer Company, serving his term in each. For two years he filled the office of secretary of the Eddy Company and he was also a trustee for two years of the same company. He is now a prominent member of the Exempt Firemen's Association. Mr. Cummings was elected to represent the Tenth Ward in the Board of Supervisors in 1882 and was reëlected the following year. His record in the Board was so creditable that his friends easily secured his nomination for coroner, to which office he was elected, served for two terms and discharged the duties with credit to himself and satisfaction to the electors of the county.

John F. Barry.

John F. Barry.

JOHN F. BARRY was born in this city September 14, 1859, the son of John and Johanna Barry. He obtained his education in the public schools. For two years he worked as a messenger boy in the office of the Western Union Telegraph Company in this city. In 1876 he was apprenticed to learn the trade of a compositor in the *Whig* office. Later he worked on the *Observer* and for five years worked in the *Times* composing room. In 1885 he embarked in the grocery business and is still in that business, having a large store at No. 728 River Street. He is the secretary of the Grocers' and Butchers' Association, is interested in the Pioneer Building-Loan Association, is a past member of the Y. M. F. M. T. A. B. Society and for eight years was a member of Typographical Union, No. 52. He was a member of the Order of Elks and was one of the original members of E. B. A., Branch 3, and in 1876 was president of the American Social Club. He was married June 26, 1883, to Miss Mary A. Lamb. They have three interesting children, two boys and a girl. Mr. Barry is one of the leading grocers of the city and commands the confidence of the business public

John H. Collins.

John H. Collins.

JOHN H. COLLINS was born November 1, 1859, in Crescent, Saratoga County. For the past twenty-one years he has been a respected and honored resident of the Tenth Ward of this city. He was educated in the public schools. Eleven years ago he started in the saloon business and has been very successful. In 1884 he was elected to represent his ward in the Board of Supervisors and was thrice reëlected. He is a member of the Emeralds, Branch 6. of the Pilsner Democratic Club and of the Edward Murphy, Jr., Steamer Company. Mr. Collins is an extremely popular young man.

William D. Cox.

William D. Cox.

WILLIAM D. COX was born in Waterford, Saratoga County, N. Y., September 11, 1859, the son of John Cox and Catherine Lanigan. His parents removed to Troy when he was very young and here he has ever since remained. He was educated at the Tenth Ward public school and at the Sisters' school. In the fall of 1886 he was elected an alderman from the Tenth Ward and in 1888 was reëlected for a term of two years. Although one of the youngest members of the Common Council, Alderman Cox is recognized as one of the most efficient and influential. He is a member of the Cleminshaw Bottling Company. Alderman Cox has been a member of the Emeralds and was one of the organizers of the Olympic Social Club. In the present Common Council he is a member of the Committees on Water-Works, Highways, Printing and Charity. Of the last mentioned committee he is chairman.

John S. Cronin.

John S. Cronin.

JOHN STEPHEN CRONIN, son of Cornelius and Mary Cronin, is a native of Troy and has always resided in this city. He was educated in the public schools, and graduated from the High School with the highest honors of his class. After leaving school Mr. Cronin became a reporter on the Troy *Press*, and was soon recognized as one of our most promising young journalists. He was attentive to his work, industrious to a degree, and it did not take him long to secure promotion to the chair of the city editor. The onerous and responsible duties of this position were ably and conscientiously discharged by Mr. Cronin. Under his careful guidance the local force of the *Press* performed wonderful work, and the paper was soon recognized as one of the newsiest in the State. For fourteen years Mr. Cronin served the paper and only left to enter business for himself. He is now a warehouseman, and has one of the largest establishments of the kind in the State, at the foot of Grand Street. The only political position ever held by Mr. Cronin, although in the days of his journalistic career he was prominent in the councils of the Democracy, was that of clerk to the Police Board, which he held for four years. In 1885 he was president of the Y. M. C. L. A. Mr. Cronin is one of Troy's substantial citizens, and possesses the confidence of the business public and the esteem of a host of friends.

Gerald G. Riordan.

Gerald G. Riordan.

GERALD G. RIORDAN was born in this city June 12, 1861, the son of John Riordan and Mary Gleason. He was educated in the public schools and by the Christian Brothers. In the High School he made a very flattering record. He studied law in the offices of Nelson Davenport and the Hon. Martin I. Townsend, and was admitted to the bar in 1881. When Mr. Townsend was United States District Attorney, Mr. Riordan acted as indictment clerk in the office, succeeding Henry Barton, who subsequently went into the diplomatic service of the United States. In 1886 Mr. Riordan opened an office of his own, entering into partnership with his gifted brother, John, who died May 29, 1889. In 1884 Mr. Riordan was admitted to practice in the United States Court by Judge Wallace at Utica, on motion of Mr. Townsend. Mr. Riordan has been remarkably successful in the practice of his profession. He is recognized as one of the best criminal lawyers in the Rensselaer County bar, and has a large and constantly increasing practice. He is an eloquent pleader, and in the preparation of a brief has few superiors.

James D. Fleming.

James D. Fleming.

JAMES D. FLEMING first saw the light of day in 1864 in this city, in the house No. 72 Federal Street. He is the son of James Fleming and Norah Holmes, and he has always resided in this city. After attending the Fourth Ward School and the High School until he had secured a splendid education he entered the employ of Peabody & Parks, and has since remained with their successors, Lockwood & Buell and T. W. Lockwood, Jr. For the first three years he served as book-keeper, and for the past five years he has been traveling for the firm, meeting with very gratifying success. Although still a young man Mr. Fleming is recognized as one of the best traveling salesmen in the State. He has acted as secretary of the Y. M. C. L. A. He is a member of the Bachelors' Club, the Pilsner Club and Post D of the Commercial Travelers.

APPENDIX.

SINCE the enclosed sketches were placed in type Senator Collins has been reëlected to the Senate for a term of two years, by an increased majority ; George O'Neil is succeeded in the Assembly by James M. Riley, and John P. Curley has retired from the civil justiceship, which he held for three terms. The appointment of District Attorney Griffith as county judge to succeed E. L. Fursman, elevated to the Supreme Court bench, rendered the office of district attorney vacant. Early in January Governor Hill filled the vacancy by the appointment of Assistant District Attorney John P. Kelly. Thomas S. Fagan, whose term as civil justice had expired, was appointed assistant district attorney. William H. Ryan has retired from his position as book-keeper in the *Press* office. Daniel T. Holland and Cornelius M. Dorsey have dissolved their partnership, and each is conducting a separate painting and decorating business. In the election last fall Mark J. Coyle was chosen an alderman from the Second Ward. Alderman Patrick J. Delaney, when the present Common Council was organized, was elected president of that body, and accordingly he is now a member of the contracting board. George E. Sands has retired from the comptroller's office, and will shortly be admitted to the bar.

FEBRUARY, 1890.

www.ingramcontent.com/pod-product-compliance
Lightning Source LLC
Chambersburg PA
CBHW021058030726
47496CB00006B/1891